SEX GUIDE

SEX GUIDE FOR MEN. THE COMPLETE GUIDE ON HOW TO HAVE SEX AND SEX POSITIONS

ROBBIE DYER

CONTENTS

Introduction v

1. Introduction to Sex and Men 1
2. Understanding Foreplay 3
3. Spicing Things Up 12
   Conclusion 16

©Copyright 2022 by Robbie Dyer
All rights Reserved

ISBN: 978-1-63970-124-7

In no way is it legal to reproduce, duplicate, or transmit any part of this document in either electronic means or in printed format. Recording of this publication is strictly prohibited and any storage of this document is not allowed unless with written permission from the publisher. All rights are reserved.
Respective authors own all copyrights not held by the publisher.

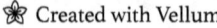 Created with Vellum

INTRODUCTION

My name is Robbie Dyer, and I once needed severe help and tips about having sex. I am extremely passionate about the contents of this book because it saved my life. I know exactly what it's like to suffer from not being a great lover.

I know the feelings of guilt, depression, and frustration after each sex experience where I wasn't at my peak state, both physical and mental, and how it was destroying my sex life.

I know what it's like not to give great sex and enjoy it, have low self-esteem, and have feelings of learned helplessness because you have tried seemingly everything out there.

This guide here is for anyone who wants to have better sex and a better, stronger bond with their partner. There is a big difference between making love and having sex, which is both the right ones depending on the outcome of your partner or your desire. This guide is for people that want to take their sex experience to a whole new level.

This book contains proven steps and strategies for having fantastic sex by teaching you how to give and receive the most unique and intense sex in your life. This is not just a book about having sex, but it will also show you how to make love to your partner most intimately and intensely possible. Many people who have been having sex and enjoying it don´t realize that they can go far beyond what they are currently capable of. So before you finish reading this book, you will know to enjoy the most fantastic sex you could have ever imagined!

I wish you the best of luck and want to thank you for downloading this book again. I am here to support you in any way that I can.

I hope you enjoy it!

Robbie Dyer

1
INTRODUCTION TO SEX AND MEN

Have you ever heard of the seven-second myth regarding men and sex? According to this myth, men think about sex every second seconds, which means it adds up to about 7200 times in a day, on the assumption that they are awake for 14 hours.

Several studies, however, refute this myth, saying 7200 times a day is an exaggeration. A study conducted at the Ohio State University revealed that, on the average, a man's thoughts are generally dominated by indulgent impulses such as sleeping and eating. As a result, he thinks about sex 19 times in a day or, going by the 14-hour-wakefulness scenario, once every 90 or so minutes.

But if we look at the results of the study of Wilhelm Hoffman, with German males as their sample, it would appear that men think about sex only once a day, taking a backseat to other "more pressing" issues such as eating, drinking, sleeping, and even personal hygiene.

Regardless of how often men think about sex, there is no escaping the fact that they DO think about it, and about doing it. But thinking and actually doing it are two different things. The most basic act of sex had always had procreation as the ultimate end, although people also view it now as a means of making a connection and experiencing pleasure.

At one point or another, every man had experienced doubts about their sexual prowess. Are they doing it right? Was it as good for their partner as it was for them? What if his partner was just forging the orgasm? Does it make the grade under the realms of "great sex"? These are only a few of the many thoughts and uncertainties that men often think about (and these thoughts probably occur every seven seconds, if that "rule" is to be believed).

Sexual satisfaction is something men strive for – both for himself and his partner – and, regardless of his level of experience on the subject and in the act itself, they can use all the help they can get.

2

UNDERSTANDING FOREPLAY

Basically, "foreplay" entails acts the man has to perform to 'prep' or get his partner ready for the sexual act. It can range from petting and kissing to all-out necking or even performing oral sex. Fortunately for men, the responsibility for foreplay no longer rests entirely on their shoulders because women also actively participate in foreplay.

While some may argue that they do not need to get primed and get it on, many deem foreplay to be necessary. It could be because they want the woman to become properly lubricated to reduce or eliminate any discomfort when the time for penetration comes. There is also the fact that some men take longer to have an erection; hence foreplay is obligatory to get "things revved up." There are also those who want to achieve maximum pleasure by drawing out the whole thing and taking as much time as possible on foreplay. According to many couples, orgasms become much more explosive after fully stimulated by well-performed and perfectly timed foreplay.

Foreplay is also the perfect excuse to relax nerves. According to Ian Kremer, writer of "She Comes First: The Thinking Man's

Guide to Pleasuring a Woman," women should be stress-free in order for them to enjoy sex. If they enjoy sex, it follows that the men will also derive great satisfaction from it.

If you are still wondering whether you should go through foreplay or not, keep in mind that women appreciate a man that takes the time to prime her up. Some men may find the interval to be quite boring and take a lot of time, but you'd feel a lot better (and more satisfied) afterward.

The Art of Kissing

Usually, the first expression of one's desire is through a kiss. Unfortunately, this is also the part that many men usually overlook, as evidenced by the great number of women who complain about the lack of kissing.

Kissing is the most effective form of foreplay, tangling and dueling tongues that mimic the sexual act you will be engaging in a little later. But don't just limit yourself to kissing your partner on the mouth. Make it a point to use your kiss and tongue action on other parts of her body, heightening the effects of the kiss by touches and caresses. The more passionate your kiss is, the more effective it will be.

Getting Started.
Sure, you may opt to skip the preliminaries and get the act done. You may derive a lot of satisfaction from that. But you are looking for great sex, and rushing things does not make for great sex.

. . .

SETTING THE MOOD.

Look at foreplay as the bottom of a road leading up to the top of the hill. You make sure the engine is warmed up, the motors are running, and then put your foot down on the accelerator for the final ascent. In foreplay, it's about setting it up.

This is the time when you can pull out all the stops in the romance department. Is the room set up for seduction and romance? Check on the lighting; are they subdued or dim enough? You don't want it to be too dark that you'd have a hard time seeing each other. Maybe put on some soft and slow music, and if there's a fireplace, stoke the fire a little to bring more warmth into the room. The moment you both walk into the room, it's not just the fire that's crackling but also the sexual tension between the two of you, waiting to be unleashed.

Light some scented candles, pour some wine on long-stemmed glasses, throw in some decadent truffles for good measure. All these will set up the scene and the mood, so there is nothing wrong with taking care of even the smallest details. Seeing a man go to such great lengths is a definite turn-on for women.

Complimenting a woman is always guaranteed to make her feel good and more drawn towards you. Tease her. Go as slow as you can. Kissing and fondling are only two of the many things you can do. Whatever you choose to do, however, make sure you do it with finesse and infinite tenderness.

FOREPLAY ACTIONS TO TAKE.

Beyond kissing, making out, and talking dirty, here are some foreplay ideas that you should try.

- Give her an oil massage, where you get to do some

sensual touching all over her body. Choose a massage oil with a subtle scent, not overpowering. The silky feel of the oil and the touch of your hands on her skin are sure to set her on fire and turn her on.

- Watch porn together. Who knows, she might even be interested in trying some of the positions you've watched when your turn comes around. Women may not say it, but they, too, love to watch porn.
- Need to knead. Do your brand of massage on her breasts and butt. Use both hands for this exercise.
- Make your finger work for you. While your tongue works on her lips and nipples, tantalize her further with some finger action down there. Push one or two fingers inside her, mimicking what you'll do with your penis later on, and you'll have her panting in no time at all. Find her G-spot with your finger, flick on her clitoris, and she's yours for the taking.
- Oral sex. Cunnilingus, or direct stimulation of the clitoris using your mouth, is also a winning foreplay idea that you should take seriously. Admittedly, not all men are keen on this. Still, hey, if you expect her to deliver a blowjob, the least you can do is return the favor. And please show some enthusiasm about it. Call it an acquired taste, but some men may need several times to practice before they get the hang of it, much less be comfortable with it. Dive in, use your tongue, your teeth. Lick, suck, bite. Do a figure-8 with your tongue. Women have different responses, so there is no template on how to perform oral sex on a woman. Feel your way through it, and trust your instincts. Also, listen to her. She may give you much-needed guidance. If you're really, really good, you

may even give her an orgasm at this point, and it's still only foreplay!

It's Not a Solo Engagement.

Sex is not an act that only one person can accomplish. It involves mutual satisfaction and gratification, and this is not restricted to the orgasm alone. The whole process, from the time your gazes locked during foreplay until you're both lying spent in each other's arms, involves more than one person. To put it bluntly, your cock is not the main character here. If you stick to this way of thinking, you will come across as self-obsessed.

Many men tend to forget about this and push forward, selfish in ensuring that they get what they want, without bothering to check if their partner is also getting as much pleasure as they are. It is highly recommended to adopt the "She comes first" attitude – literally and figuratively. Take care of her pleasure first before taking care of your own. You'll feel more fulfilled that way.

There are women who are turned on by dirty talk from their male partners. On the other hand, there are others who feel even more relaxed when told that they look and taste great. Of course, not all women are comfortable when men go down on them, but it's guaranteed to be an equally pleasurable experience for both with the right words and the right timing.

Communication is very important between two people about to engage in what they hope to be amazing sex. Small talk, deep conversation, it doesn't matter. Women find conversations to be very strong aphrodisiacs.

When in doubt, ask. There is nothing wrong with a man asking his partner what she wants during intercourse. It will give the woman a degree of control or power over the act, turning her on even further, knowing that you are taking the time out to pleasure her in the way she wants.

GETTING IN POSITION.

Whether you want it slow and intimate or you prefer wild and fast, there are many sexual positions that you can do to ensure satisfaction for you both. Many men have made the Kama Sutra their sex "bible," studying the positions and incorporating them in their sex lives. Here are some of the many sexual positions guaranteed to give you – and your partner – a mind-blowing orgasm.

MISSIONARY.

Hey, don't knock the Missionary position. Probably the most underrated of all sexual positions, the Missionary remains a surefire way to achieve orgasm without severing that intimate contact. And don't just stick to the in-and-out thrusting motion, either. Slow figure-eight movements with your hips set up the perfect buildup to a powerful orgasm.

Modification: Prop up her butt by putting a couple of pillows underneath her, and hold her arms high over her head to keep her body fully open.

BUTTERFLY.

Stand or kneel on the floor against the side of the bed, pull her towards your groin so her butt is hanging over the edge, and you're kneeling between her legs. You get a full-frontal view as you enter her and you can even add manual stimulation while you're at it. This position guarantees deep penetration.

Modification: This is also a good position when used on the

edge of a couch, table, counter, or pool! For added stimulation, have her wrap her legs around your hips.

Deep Impact.

Just like the Butterfly position, the woman will be on her back, with her butt hanging on the edge of the bed, and you in a kneeling place between her splayed legs. Lift her legs and rest them on your shoulders, then enter her fully. Penetration is deeper in this position, and you can bury yourself to the hilt. However, those who are quite big should be more cautious since it can be quite painful for the woman.

Modification: Instead of kneeling, switch to a standing position and lift her butt with her hands. This is also known as the Down-stroke position. It does not penetrate as deep, but with the right maneuvering of her hips and timing of your thrusts, it's as deeply satisfying.

Doggy Style.

With her on all fours on the floor or on the bed, hold her hips to be steady her (and keep you balanced) as you enter her from behind. To make the angle more pleasurable for you both, you can have her lower her breasts on the floor, with her butt high up in the air for your penetration. This is perfect for hitting the G-spot, and you can experiment with your hip movements to draw out the pleasure even more.

Modification: Push her feet close together and, instead of kneeling, get up on a crouch, with your knees on each side of her hips.

Spoon.

The Spoon position is a highly sensual one. Make her lie down on her side and take position behind her. Assume a half-kneeling position, keeping your knees half-bent, lift her top leg, and enter her from behind. The great thing about this position is how it allows multiple stimulations: penetration and, since your hands are free, you can touch her anywhere.

Modification: Lift her butt so halfway, so it's a half-doggy half-kneeling spoon position. Snatching deep tongue kisses won't hurt at all, either.

FLOOR SHOW.

Have her stand in front of you, her back to your front, then bend her forward until she touches the floor with her hands. Then, enter her from behind at a downward angle, hitting her sweet spot.

Modification: Try the Prison Guard position. Instead of her hands on the floor, pull back her wrists as if they are in handcuffs.

COWGIRL.

Women love it when you concede control to them from time to time. The best way to do that is to let her be on top and ride you. You can have her do it while kneeling or with her feet planted beside you. You can look into each other's eyes while she rides you, and you can even put your fingers to work.

MODIFICATION.

The Reverse cowgirl position is also a favorite because of its angle for hitting the G-spot. Instead of her facing you, have her face the ceiling, with her butt slapping your groin as she goes up and down.

These are only a few of the many sex positions you can use in your repertoire. Do not be afraid to experiment. Remember, you should look for what gives you both the most pleasure, so there's no need to go by the book. Just do what makes you both feel amazingly good.

3
SPICING THINGS UP

How do you go about spicing up your sex life?

Variety. The phrase "variety is the spice of life" can be restated as "variety is the spice of your sex life". Perhaps you and your partner are used to certain sexual positions; try something new. But, of course, you have to ease into it. You do not want to spring it on your partner suddenly. She may not be comfortable with the suddenness of it.

Be adventurous. So you are used to doing it on a bed or the couch. Ever tried doing it against the door? In the tub? What about the narrow shower stall? You might want to put that new dinner table to the test and see if it can hold a lot of weight. Stairwells also make for some challenging but extremely satisfying positions. Some even go to the extent of having sex in public places. I won't tell you not to do that, but when you do, make sure it won't lead to problems such as being arrested for indecent acts or exposure.

Be spontaneous. Maybe you've been sticking to a certain schedule on when to have sex. For example, you've gotten used to doing it only at night. Ever tried early morning sex? Wake her up for some early morning action. Or, during lunch hour, send her a dirty text and ask her to meet you in a hotel room for an afternoon quickie.

Striptease. It's not just the women who should do this. Women are also turned on when their men do a slow and sensual striptease in front of them.

Accessorize. Instead of having sex naked, do it with just your tie and her wearing heels. Or you could even employ the use of sex toys to up the ante even more.

KEEPING IT UP.

HOW OFTEN SHOULD **you have sex?**

According to sex expert Michael Castleman, couples committed to a healthy, stable relationship have sex at least once every ten days. But how often can a man have sex?

Several factors come into play here. Is he in a committed relationship, or is he single? Is he looking for something permanent, or is he simply content to have flings now and then? Normally, married men have sex twice a week; a single guy once a week, or even less. Those who play the field, however, see more action.

OVERCOMING PERFORMANCE ANXIETY.

Men are often plagued by performance anxiety when it comes to sex, especially when their partners are not forthcoming about how they feel about the whole experience. The fact that women confess to having faked an orgasm a time or two does not help matters.

You should recognize that sex is not a performance, where you are given a role that you must adhere to.

Most of the men's insecurities come from hearing other men talk about how great they are in the sack and even from watching seemingly perfect male specimens with the ideal package do a stellar job. Do not let yourself get affected by locker room stories; chances are, they are having the same problems. They are just better at hiding it.

As for porn, you should remember that the male porn stars are in a performance and have roles to portray. Do not use pornography as your teacher or compare your sex life with the porn videos you watch in the privacy of your room. They are actors acting out what is written on a script; you are involved with reality. So take some cues from it, but do not expect the results to be the same.

Additional Tips for Men
What Not to Do.

Do not fixate on your shortcomings, but concentrate on your strengths. Contrary to what they say, size does not matter much. When it comes down to it, sex does not come down to the size or if you and your partner fit. Instead, recognize where you lack and make up for it in an area you are good at. You may be of modest size, but when you know how to hit her sweet spot, you can be sure that size will be the last thing on her mind. Remember, skill also factors a lot.

Do not think all women are the same, especially when it comes to pleasing them. Women's sexuality is quite complicated, mainly because every woman responds differently to sensations. As a result, women have varied preferences regarding sexual positions, rhythm, depth, and other sex-related issues.

What to Do.

Do stay fit and healthy. Stamina and physical fitness play vital roles in your sex life. Work out regularly and stay away from elements that can potentially harm your health. If you want to have staying power and deliver a sterling performance in bed (or out of it), making sure you are in top condition is essential.

Do eat right. According to Great Food, Great Sex co-author Dr. Lynn Edlen-Nezin, men should stick to foods rich in Arginine, which is the basis of the drug Viagra. These include oysters and fish, greens and beans, as well as other lean proteins.

Do you know who you're having sex with. Calling out another woman's name during foreplay or the actual intercourse itself is not just a mood-breaker. It is also of poor taste and puts you in a bad light.

DO PRACTICE SAFE SEX. Always. It's not just about avoiding accidental pregnancies and sexually transmitted infections. It is also a way of showing your partner that you respect her. Take regular medical checkups and, unless you are trying for a baby, do not forget to use protection whenever you engage in the act. You're not just protecting yourself; you are also protecting your partner.

The important thing to remember throughout all these is that sex is a shared experience meant to be savored and enjoyed. Have fun; do not stress over it. Yes, it is important, but it should not be the be-all and end-all. Masculinity should not be measured entirely on your prowess beneath the sheets. A huge part of sex involves the mind, not just the body. Use both, and you will no doubt be the great lover that you have always aspired to be.

CONCLUSION

Thank you again for downloading this book!

I hope this book was able to help you to take your sex life to a new level by giving you insights that have changed your life and helping you be more confident and happy.

The next step is to keep on getting better every day by applying these ideas and concepts and evolving yourself into the ideal you.

Finally, if you enjoyed this book, I'd like to ask you for a favor. Would you be kind enough to leave a review for this book on Amazon? It'd be greatly appreciated!

www.ingramcontent.com/pod-product-compliance
Lightning Source LLC
LaVergne TN
LVHW021751060526
838200LV00052B/3577